What readers are saying about *In 30 Minutes* guides.

Dropbox In 30 Minutes

"I was intimidated by the whole idea of storing my files in the cloud, but **this book took me through the process and made it so easy.**"

"**This was truly a 30-minute tutorial** and I have mastered the basics without bugging my 20-year-old son! Yahoo!"

"**Very engaging and witty.**"

Google Drive & Docs In 30 Minutes

"I bought your Google Docs guide myself (my new company uses it) and it was really handy. **I loved it.**"

"I have been impressed by the writing style and how easy it was to get very familiar and start leveraging Google Docs. **I can't wait for more titles.** Nice job!"

Twitter In 30 Minutes

"A perfect introduction to Twitter. **Quick and easy read with lots of photos.** I finally understand the # symbol!"

"Clarified any issues and concerns I had and **listed some excellent precautions**."

Excel Basics In 30 Minutes

"**Fast and easy, this book is everything it claims to be**. The material presented is very basic but it is also incredibly accessible with step-by-step screenshots and a friendly tone more like a friend or co-worker explaining how to use Excel than a technical manual."

"**An excellent little guide**. For those who already know their way around Excel, it'll be a good refresher course. For those who don't, it's a clear, easy-to-follow handbook of time-saving and stress-avoiding skills in Excel. Definitely plan on passing it around the office."

LinkedIn In 30 Minutes

"**This book does everything it claims**. It gives you a great introduction to LinkedIn and gives you tips on how to make a good profile."

"I already had a LinkedIn account, which I use on a regular basis, but still found the book very helpful. The author gave examples and explained why it is important to detail and promote your account. **Reading this book has motivated me to return to my account** and update it to make it more thorough and attention-grabbing."

Learn more about *In 30 Minutes*® guides at **in30minutes.com**

Twitter In 30 Minutes

How to connect with interesting people, write great tweets, and find information that's relevant to you.

Second Edition

By Ian Lamont

Contents

Introduction

One January afternoon, I saw a remarkable event unfold on Twitter.

It was around 3:30 p.m., and I was sitting at my desk. A few people I followed on Twitter suddenly began sending out short text messages (called *tweets*) about a plane crash. The plane had apparently gone down in New York City, right in the Hudson River. New Yorkers in nearby buildings had seen the crash, or spotted a plane floating in the river, and were sharing scraps of information in the short, 140-character text messages that Twitter allows.

I checked CNN and Google News. There were no official news reports. Yet people on the ground were reporting a disaster. What was going on?

Then I saw someone share a remarkable photograph on Twitter:

The photo showed survivors standing on the wing, or stepping into a boat. The tweet that accompanied the photo said:

> *There's a plane in the Hudson. I'm on the ferry going to pick up the people. Crazy.*

I did not know Janis Krums, the person who took the photo from a passing ferry. But the photo and short message he posted on Twitter indicated that many passengers were alive, and were in the process of being rescued. Krums' friends shared the message, which was shared again with thousands of other people. Considering there was no official report or news account of what was happening, it was reassuring to see Krums' tweet.

The story of US Airways Flight 1549 is now well known, thanks to the quick thinking and professionalism of Capt. Chesley B. "Sully" Sullenberger and his crew. More than 150 people were on the plane when it ran into a flock of geese and made an emergency water landing on the Hudson River. It could have been a tragedy. Yet every passenger survived.

But the incident was important for another reason: It showed that Twitter is more than just a collection of fleeting observations about everyday life. Twitter can connect people to events, information and each other in ways that have never been experienced before.

What is Twitter?

Twitter is a free tool that can connect you with interesting people, events and information. Twitter is available online at *twitter.com*, or as a free app that can be installed on a mobile phone or tablet. Millions of people all over the world consider Twitter to be as important to their daily communications routines as checking their email, sending text messages, or catching up with friends on Facebook.

How do people use Twitter? Here are some examples:

- **Abby** (@AbbyLeighTaylor) is an Oklahoma native now living in Nashville. She loves using Twitter to connect with people who share her interests in music and Mexican food.

- **Fiona** (@EmeraldFaerie), a jewelry designer based in London, uses Twitter to show off her latest creations, and let customers know where they can be purchased.

- **The New York Public Library** (@nypl) tweets about library programs, author appearances, photographs from its archives, and even job openings.

- **Steven** (@IamStevenT) is none other than Steven Tyler, the hard-rock singer and TV personality. On Twitter, he talks about his tour schedule and television appearances, and also uses Twitter to connect with fans.

- **Todd** (@sweendogg1070) is a father, teacher, and sports fanatic (Buffalo Bills, Buffalo Sabres, and New York Yankees). He uses Twitter to talk about sports with other fans and ask questions related to his favorite teams.

- **Mark** (@mcuban) is a famous entrepreneur who uses Twitter to promote his business interests and basketball team, the Dallas Mavericks. He also answers questions from fans and offers support to people who have seen him on TV or have read his book or blog.

- **James** (@JamesBondTheDog) is the self-proclaimed "international hound dog of mystery." Like many parody accounts on Twitter, the focus is on humor ("Apple, you showed a squirrel at your press conference. You have my attention."). Many of James' followers are pet owners who have created Twitter accounts for their dogs.

As you can see from these examples, there are all kinds of people, organizations and interests represented on Twitter. Further, they use Twitter for varied purposes — connecting with like-minded people, promoting their businesses or causes, and having fun.

However, Twitter can be bewildering to newbies. The messages are short. There are strange symbols and unfamiliar conventions. It may not be apparent how Twitter can help you connect with people or start conversations.

The second edition of this guide is intended to help you get your bearings and teach you how to get the most out of Twitter. *Twitter In 30 Minutes* concentrates on core skills and use cases that a beginner should understand. In the next 30 minutes, you'll learn how to do everything from setting up and personalizing your account online or using a mobile phone (Chapter 2), to finding interesting people to follow (Chapter 3). There's a chapter that discusses how to tweet (Chapter 4). You'll even learn a few tricks, ranging from hashtags to retweeting (Chapter 5).

What can Twitter do for you?

At its heart, Twitter lets you do three things:

1. **Broadcast to the world what you are doing, what you are thinking, and who you are with**. The broadcasts are short messages called *tweets* that contain no more than 140 characters of text. It's also possible to add a photograph or a link to a news story. While anyone can see these tweets, the messages are most likely to be noticed by people who *follow* you on Twitter.

2. **Monitor what other people are saying and doing**. Millions of ordinary people — as well as companies, schools, sports teams, charities, politicians and superstars — broadcast their own messages to the world. You can choose to follow the accounts of people you like or who you think are interesting. When you follow someone, you will be able to see his or her recent tweets. Some may even follow you back, to see what you have to say!

3. **Learn about the world**. Because people all over the world use Twitter to describe what they are doing, how they are feeling, and what they are seeing, Twitter is a window into events, opinions, and information. Want to know what other people think about the latest episode of your favorite TV show or sports team? Want to see photographs taken at a concert, beach, or political rally? Twitter can let you do that. The flow of information is sometimes rough, but it

grants an unfiltered view of the world, often before "official" sources weigh in.

In the following chapters, you'll learn how to follow people, write tweets, and engage in other activities. We only have 30 minutes, so let's get started!

CHAPTER ONE

A brief tour of Twitter

Before I show you how to sign up for Twitter and start using the service, let's take a brief tour of Twitter to better understand how people use it. We'll start with a famous person (Oprah Winfrey), move onto a Twitter account operated by a local business, and then see how ordinary people use Twitter.

@Oprah

If you are sitting near a computer, or have a mobile phone, open a Web browser and type *twitter.com/oprah* into the address bar. This is the Web address for Oprah Winfrey, the talented American television host, actress, and media mogul. If you are sitting at a desktop computer, you will see something like this:

There's a lot going on. Photos and seemingly random messages litter the page. Elsewhere there are references to *Tweets, Followers,* and *Following,* along with numbers. There are buttons and strange symbols. There's also a photo of Oprah. What's happening here?

Think of *twitter.com/oprah* as Oprah's public display case. She (and her staff) determine nearly everything seen on this page. Most of the action takes place in the center of the screen. On the left side of the page, you can see Oprah's name and her Twitter name, or "handle" — @Oprah (pronounced "at-Oprah").

The front page of the @Oprah Twitter account also includes photos of Oprah, which often come from her magazine. She regularly changes the profile picture, and sometimes uses funny or striking images. Once she featured a photo of herself with a giant Afro. It looked outlandish, but Oprah has a sense of humor and that's what she wants her fans to see!

Below this are some numbers corresponding to *tweets*, *following*, and *followers*. Here's what the numbers mean:

- **Tweets**: A tweet is a message that is no more than 140 characters in length. Oprah has sent out more than 9,000 such messages. This seems like a lot. However, she has been using Twitter for years. Considering each message takes less than a minute to compose, it's not hard to create more than one thousand tweets in a single year. Oprah's most recent tweets are shown at the top of the page. If you keep scrolling down, Oprah's older tweets will be revealed.

- **Following**: This number refers to other Twitter accounts that Oprah follows. There are relatively few people on the list. If you click on the number, you will see who they are. Most are media personalities, guests who have appeared on her show, and her staff. When one of them tweets something, Oprah will see it when she visits *twitter.com* or opens the Twitter app on her phone.

- **Followers**: Oprah has lots of fans, and more than 25 million of them have chosen to "follow" Oprah on Twitter. This means they will see Oprah's tweets when they look at Twitter, along with any other accounts they are following. Following a Twitter account is kind of like "friending" someone on Facebook, except it's only one-way. In other words, you can follow people on Twitter, but unlike Facebook, they don't have to follow you back. In Oprah's case, millions of people are following her, but she doesn't have to reciprocate.

Below this info are Oprah's most recent tweets. What is she talking about? Let's take a look:

Oprah Winfrey @Oprah · May 9
.@BrentALong your mom will love spending time with you..and hopefully me too :) Can't wait to see you! #LifeYouWantTour

57   129   ···   View conversation

Oprah Winfrey @Oprah · May 8
Its the hardest job on earth. Mother's Day, bring your mom to @Starbucks for a special treat on me #EveryMomGetsAChai bit.ly /1j7FymK

934   987   ···

Oprah Winfrey @Oprah · May 8
.@jtimberlake Btw I love the way you self reflect. We see you're talented and Wise. #MasterClass

249   666   ···   View conversation

It may seem jarring to see these tiny fragments of unrelated conversations on someone's Twitter profile. That's just the nature of Twitter. Later, we'll learn how to expand these conversations and even join them.

What can Oprah's tweets tell us about her interests and activities? First, she frequently engages with the people and companies she supports, such as pop star Justin Timberlake (@jtimberlake) and Starbucks Coffee (@Starbucks).

Second, Oprah uses Twitter to promote her entertainment empire. Because she has so many followers on Twitter, mentioning or endorsing something is an extremely powerful promotional tool. Sometimes these products or ideas are associated with *hashtags*, which are words or phrases preceded by the pound symbol. In Chapter 5, we will learn more about hashtags. In the tweets shown above, the hashtags are specific to Oprah's businesses and partnerships. For example, *#LifeYouWantTour* is a reference to Oprah's live tour of various U.S. cities featuring her "life trailblazers." *#MasterClass* references a popular program on Oprah's cable television channel. Justin Timberlake was a recent guest on the program.

In terms of Oprah's popularity on Twitter, it should be noted that the @Oprah account is unusual. Oprah was famous *before* she joined Twitter, and has her own television network, which explains her army of followers.

This is rare. Very few people and organizations have this level of influence on Twitter. It's far more common to have just a few hundred followers. As you might expect, having a few hundred followers vs. millions of followers changes the nature of the discussions and interactions on Twitter.

@Momogoose

For our second example, we're going to look at a local business. Momogoose operates food trucks and cafes in the Boston area. I discovered the food trucks when I was a grad student, and was surprised to see they had a Twitter handle — @momogoose — painted on the exterior of the trucks. What could a food truck possibly have to say on Twitter?

A lot, it turns out. Here's *twitter.com/momogoose*:

Like Oprah, Momogoose uses Twitter for promotional purposes and reaching out to fans. But the scale is much smaller. Momogoose only has a few thousand followers, and most of them are in the Boston area. Why do these people follow a food truck on Twitter? Obviously, they like the trucks and the food, and following @momogoose on Twitter is a way of showing support. But it's also a way of finding out about Momogoose, the business.

Indeed, @momogoose sends out a regular stream of tweets on weekdays describing new dishes or specials. Based on these tweets, some followers may decide to visit one of the trucks. Even if the result is only two or three additional sales per day, that adds up over time. For Momogoose, Twitter is a free promotional tool that can help attract customers and generate revenue.

Momogoose also uses Twitter to connect with customers and other businesses in other ways. Some Twitter users ask questions, while others give feedback. @Momogoose is only too happy to engage with its customers using Twitter. Momogoose also follows many of its fans, as well as other local businesses.

@RobertFischer

Robert Fischer may not be a celebrity, but he is a very active person on Twitter, with tens of thousands of tweets. Here is his profile, located at *twitter.com/RobertFischer*:

As you can see from his profile, @RobertFischer puts his interests front and center for other people to see. This helps potential followers decide whether or not to follow him.

The topics @RobertFischer tweets about run the gamut from bluegrass to programming to politics. Every now and then, he'll throw out a link to a funny video. He is very engaged with the people he follows and his followers — he frequently responds to questions or comments on Twitter, and also uses it to ask questions related to software development and other topics.

@Jus_Tish

Like @RobertFisher, @Jus_Tish is a normal person (as opposed to a celebrity) using Twitter to talk about her interests and reach out to friends. Here's her profile page at *twitter.com/jus_tish*:

One thing that's worth noting: The identity of @Jus_Tish is not entirely clear. While she has a profile photo, she chose to use a nickname for her Twitter handle, and does not reveal any information about her hometown or occupation. Twitter asks all new users to enter a full name when they register, but it's also possible to use nicknames, initials and fanciful identities. Anonymous or semi-anonymous Twitter identities give people more flexibility in terms of what they say and how they present themselves.

What does @Jus_Tish tweet about? She loves going to church. She likes music — about half of her tweets relate to something she's listening to or watching on YouTube. She actively participates in discussions about one of her favorite singers, Calvin Richardson (@ThePrinceOfSoul). She likes Chinese food, and sometimes talks about what she is watching on TV. @Jus_Tish also reaches out to a small circle of Twitter connections to offer reassurance, updates or observations about life. Her tweets are sprinkled with great quotes.

@Jus_Tish tweets a lot. In a typical day, Tish sends dozens of tweets. How can she do it? She uses the Twitter app on her phone. This allows her to tweet from practically anywhere.

@Caliguy16

There is one last Twitter account I want to use as an example. Here's the account for @caliguy16:

As you start to use Twitter, you will see many accounts that have an image of an egg instead of a person or logo. Why the egg? If someone starts an account but doesn't provide a profile picture, then Twitter will default to a graphic of an egg on a colored background. The different colors don't mean anything, but the egg is associated with "newbie" accounts, belonging to people who just got started with Twitter or those who abandoned the accounts not long after registering them. Indeed, @caliguy16 tweeted twice (in 2008) and then abandoned Twitter.

It's not clear why @caliguy16 gave up. If I were to hazard a guess, I would point to the lack of a network. He never followed anyone and was followed by only one person — a local politician who barely used Twitter himself. Because @caliguy16 did not follow anyone, this means there would have been no information or people to talk with in his timeline. If you don't build your network, Twitter will seem like a lonely and boring place.

I also want to mention something about the egg icon. While there's nothing wrong with being a newbie on Twitter, there's no excuse for being represented by an egg. Egg profiles send negative signals to other people on Twitter, who may avoid following accounts that don't appear very dedicated to the Twitter community.

Fortunately, it's easy enough to create and upload a profile picture using your phone or *twitter.com*. I'll show you how to do this in the next chapter.

CHAPTER TWO

Signing up for Twitter

There are two ways to sign up for Twitter: online (using a Web browser on your PC or laptop), or on a mobile device (such as a phone or tablet). Both ways are easy. I recommend registering online, using a desktop or laptop computer, because you are less likely to make a typing mistake (important for usernames and passwords).

How to register online

Open up your Web browser, and type *twitter.com* into the address bar. You should see something like this:

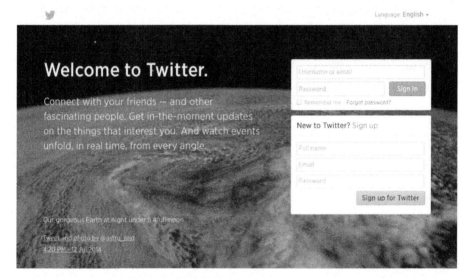

To create a Twitter account, you only need to submit a valid email address and password. The email address is required to confirm the account, and is also used to send you notifications and other messages. You can leave the name field blank, but later you will have to add something, even if it's a fake name, a nickname, or initials.

Here's the next screen:

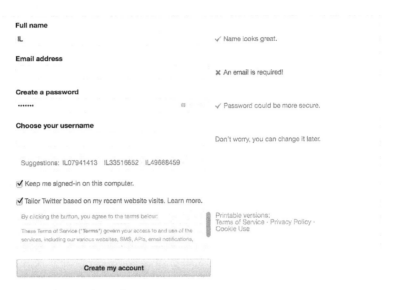

There are a few fields worth noting:

Name: If you left it blank on the first screen, you will have to fill it in here. You don't have to use your real name, and you can change it later. For the sake of this example, I will put in my initials, "IL," before pressing the continue button.

Username: This string of letters and numbers will become my Twitter handle. But there's a problem — Twitter has suggested I choose IL07941413 as a username. I don't want to have @IL07941413 as my Twitter handle, as it's hard to remember. Twitter also suggests IL33516652 and IL49668459, which are just as bad. I want something that is more personal or relates to my company. The username "ian" is already taken, but the username "author_ianl" is available. So my Twitter handle will be @author_ianl.

Some people like to use Twitter usernames that are similar to their real names. For instance, the singer Alicia Keys uses @aliciakeys while Bob Dylan has @bobdylan. My personal Twitter account, which I have used since 2007, is @ilamont. Handles like this are easy to remember, but some people don't want to directly connect their identities to Twitter. What's more, it's difficult to choose handles based on common names, because other people may have already chosen them.

Twitter allows people to change their usernames, but I advise picking a username you like and sticking with it.

Keep me signed in: If this is a computer that only you use, keep this box checked. If it's the family computer, or a public computer at a library or school, keep it blank, or anyone else who has access to the browser may be able to post tweets on your account. This can be embarrassing or even cause real trouble.

Tailor Twitter based on my recent website visits: Checking this box lets Twitter monitor many of the sites that you visit, and display advertisements and other content based on what you've viewed on other websites. Imagine what sorts of assumptions Twitter will make based on the sites your 7-year-old son checks out, or the fact that you once looked up the Home Depot website to see what time the nearest branch closes. Twitter may assume you love Legos and riding mowers, and will mercilessly bombard you with such ads. My advice: Leave this box unchecked.

Once you have made your choices, click the *Create My Account* button.

Follow recommended accounts

After creating your handle, you will be brought to a quick tutorial that explains what tweets are and why you should follow other people.

Twitter is a social network. Not only can you create 140-character tweets and post photos, you are also supposed to follow other people — friends, strangers, celebrities, businesses, and even @JamesBondTheDog. Following their Twitter accounts lets you see the tweets that they create, which shows their interests and daily lives.

Twitter wants you to start following people right away, and asks you to follow a small number of accounts from a list of recommended accounts. If you are a teenager, you might find the suggestions appealing — the list is dominated by the latest pop stars and television personalities:

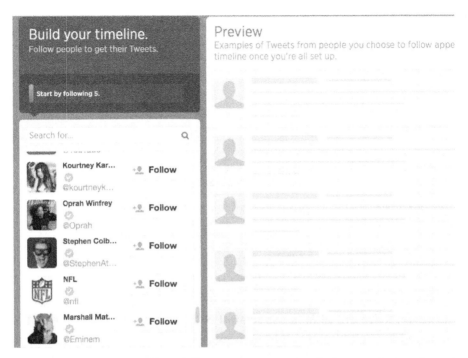

You'll then be prompted to follow even more people from category-based lists. There are celebrities, but Twitter also presents other categories, such as people in technology, politics, fashion, health, and religion. There are also accounts for charitable organizations and news services. Follow @RedCross, @Smithsonian, @NYTimes, @DalaiLama, @Pontifex (the Twitter handle for Pope Francis), and any other accounts that strike your fancy. Twitter's recommendations are mostly famous accounts with lots of followers. You'll have a chance to follow ordinary folks later.

Upload contact lists to Twitter

The next screen requires some care to navigate. Twitter will help you find friends to follow by looking at the email addresses in your Yahoo, Gmail, or Hotmail contact lists and matching them up with existing Twitter accounts, which are then recommended to you.

I have mixed feelings about this service. On the one hand, it's a very convenient way to find friends and colleagues with Twitter accounts, even if they are using an obscure Twitter handle. For instance, a few dozen people showed up on the left side of the screen when I let Twitter sync to my Yahoo account:

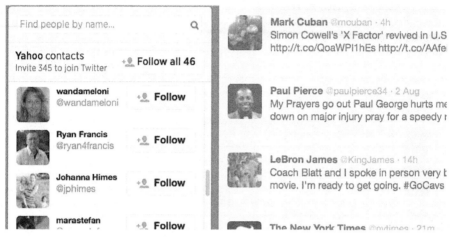

However, there are pitfalls associated with letting Twitter gather all the email addresses in your address book. For instance, did you notice the *Invite 345 to join Twitter* link? If I click it, Twitter will spam 345 of my other Yahoo contacts who are not on Twitter. No thanks!

In addition, Twitter may use the data for other purposes, from building profiles of new users based on their address book connections to targeting people with certain types of advertisements. It's spammy, and you have little control over how Twitter uses the data.

Because of Twitter's spammy practices, most users should avoid syncing their address books to Twitter. If you *do* decide to sync your address book to Twitter, only use it to find friends. Refrain from inviting everyone in your address book to Twitter by clicking the barely noticeable *Skip* link near the bottom of the left column. If you are prompted again to invite all of the contacts in your address book, click the "X" on the pop-up prompt.

Add a profile photo and bio to your Twitter profile

You'll be brought to a screen that lets you customize two basic profile elements: your profile photo and bio. Take a few minutes to complete this step online or using Twitter's mobile app.

Failing to upload a photo will result in a profile marked by an egg graphic, similar to the one belonging to @caliguy16 in Chapter 1. Egg accounts send a signal to other people that you don't know how to use Twitter, or have abandoned the social network. Egg accounts are less likely to be followed.

Here's what the Profile settings page looks like:

Click the *Upload* button to find a photo on your hard drive. Most people use recent headshots, but photos from old photo albums or photos of pets are common.

The bio has to be less than 140 characters. You may want to use funny descriptors ("Sharp-dressed taco aficionado and die-hard Eagles fan") or something more down-to-earth ("Real estate lawyer serving greater Phoenix"). I chose something in between, with a cute picture of myself at age 4, and a tame message about what I do and what I like ("Author of In 30 Minutes guides. Cat lover.")

Note you can change your profile photo and bio at any time, by clicking the Settings icon on *twitter.com* and selecting *Edit Profile*.

You can also customize other elements of your profile, including header and background images.

Add a header photo

Looking at my profile, there's one more thing I want to customize. Notice the blank area above my most recent tweets? It's possible (but not required) to place a header photo there. To do so, follow these steps:

1. Click the gear-like Settings icon in the upper right corner of the browser window, and select *Settings*.

2. On the left side of the screen, select *Profile*.

3. Click the *Change Header* button and browse your hard drive for the photo you want to use.

4. Twitter recommends an image that is 1500 pixels wide and 500 pixels tall. Don't worry if you don't know what a pixel is or how to get the image to fit these dimensions. Twitter will let you crop or zoom in on a normal-sized photo.

5. Click the *Apply* button.

6. You will be brought back to the Profile settings page. Scroll to the bottom and click *Save Changes*.

Here's what my profile looks like with a landscape header image:

If you decide to replace the profile picture or header photo, go to the Profile settings and follow the steps listed above.

Confirm your Twitter account registration

Once you've created an account, you'll be prompted to confirm your registration. Go to the email account you used to register for Twitter, and look for the email from Twitter that says "Confirm your account."

IL,
Please confirm your Twitter account

Confirming your account will give you **full access to Twitter** and all future notifications will be sent to this email address.

Confirm your account now

Or click the link below:
https://twitter.com/account/confirm_email/author_ianl/73EFB-5B28F-140739

Forgot your Twitter password? Get instructions on how to reset it.
If you received this message in error and did not sign up for Twitter, click not my account.
Twitter, Inc. 1355 Market St., Suite 900 San Francisco, CA 94103

Click the button or the link. Your account will be confirmed! You are ready to start following other people (Chapter 3) and tweeting (Chapter 4).

How to register using a phone or tablet

Registering on a mobile phone or tablet is quick. Twitter makes apps for most mobile platforms, including:

- **Android**: Phones and tablets from Samsung, Motorola, Xiaomi, Nexus, and many others.
- **iOS**: The iPhone, iPad, and iPod touch
- **BlackBerry phones**
- **Windows-based phones and tablets**
- **Other devices,** including the Apple Watch and some Nokia handsets

In this section, I'll cover Android and iOS devices, which dominate the market. The Twitter app can be downloaded via Apple's App Store and Google Play. Setup processes are nearly identical. If you have a Windows Phone, BlackBerry, or another device, go to *twitter.com/download* to get the app.

How to install Twitter on Android

1. Open Google Play on your Android device (phone, tablet, etc.) and search for Twitter.
2. Tap the *Install* button.
3. If you are prompted with a security warning that Twitter is attempting to access your contact list, tap the *Deny* button.
4. Open the app.

You will see something like this:

Hello. Welcome to Twitter.

Ian Lamont

Create my account

Sign up a different account   Sign In

There are several options to start using the Twitter app. If you already have a Twitter account that you created online, tap the *Sign In* button and enter your Twitter username and password. If you do not have a Twitter account, follow these steps:

1. Press the *Create My Account* button. You will be prompted to create a new Twitter account associated with your Google account used with Google Play.

2. You can also click the *Sign up a different account* link to create a Twitter account from scratch.

3. The next screen (see screenshot, below) will autofill the name and email address from your Google account, and will suggest a Twitter username. Or, you can enter other values, but your email address and username cannot already be in use on Twitter.

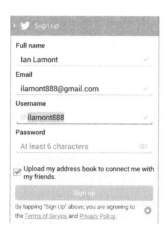

Before you press the *Sign Up* button, take note of the *Upload my address book to connect me with my friends* checkbox. According to Twitter's Privacy Policy, this allows Twitter to copy the contacts on your phone and take the following actions:

1. Match the address book information with friends who already have Twitter accounts, and suggest that you follow them.

2. Urge you to spam everyone on else in your address book with messages to sign up for Twitter.

3. Use the address book information to make it easier for other people to find you on Twitter.

Because of the spammy nature of Twitter's use of address book data, I recommend new users *not* upload their address books to Twitter. There are other ways to connect with friends on Twitter, as outlined in Chapter 3.

The first time you log into the Twitter app, you may be asked if you want to let Twitter access location data on your phone. This basically means Twitter wants to know where you are. This data might be appended to tweets and photos you distribute. If you are sensitive about privacy and tracking, do not accept this option.

How to install Twitter on an iPhone or iPad

The Twitter apps for the iPhone and iPad look great, and generally perform very well, thanks to the standard iOS interfaces and powerful Apple hardware.

Registering for Twitter on your iPhone or iPad is easy:

1. Open the Apple App Store, and download the Twitter app.

2. Once installed, press the *Sign Up* button (press the *Sign In* button if you have already created an account online).

3. On the next screen, enter your name (or initials), email address, username, and password. Note that your username must be unique to Twitter.

4. Press the blue button to create your account.

The app will ask if it can access the contact list on your iOS device. Agreeing to this will let Twitter match the email addresses in your contact list with existing Twitter accounts.

Because of Twitter's spammy policies around the use of users' address books, I recommend users reject the app's requests to access this data. There will be other ways to connect with friends and interesting people, as described later in this guide.

Mobile recommendations

Once you are signed into Twitter on your tablet or phone, you may be prompted to follow accounts belonging to other people:

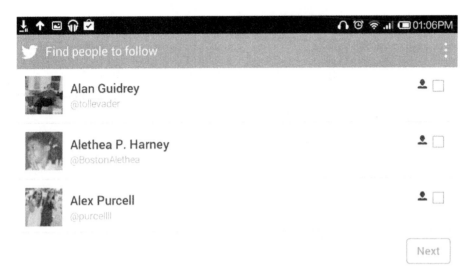

Some will be accounts belonging to famous people or high-profile organizations. Others will be strangers. A few accounts may belong to friends or other people you know, including friends and colleagues.

How does Twitter know that you are connected? Even if you followed my advice earlier in this chapter and did *not* upload your address book to Twitter, other people you know may have uploaded *their* address books, which may include your name and email address. Twitter will therefore know you are connected, and will recommend their Twitter accounts to you on this screen.

You can find other friends to follow using the instructions given later in this guide.

Add photos and a bio using the Twitter app

The Twitter app for phones and tablets will prompt new users to customize their profiles with photos and a brief bio. Using your phone to add a Twitter profile or header photo is quite convenient, as you can use selfies and other photos taken with the phone's camera.

For instance, new Twitter users on Android will be prompted with this view of their profiles:

Tap the pencil icons to change the profile and header photos, or tap the description field to change your bio.

How to change your profile using the Twitter app

If you have already created a Twitter profile, but want to change the photo or bio using the Twitter app, here's how to do it:

Android:

Open the Android app, click the More Settings icon (three dots in the upper right corner of the screen), and tap your Twitter handle:

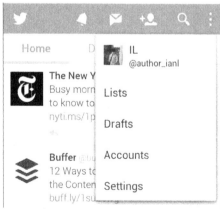

iPhone or iPad:

1. Open the app, and click the Me icon (lower right corner of the screen)

2. Click the gear icon below your profile photo

3. Select *Edit Profile*

4. Tap *Photo* or *Header* to make changes

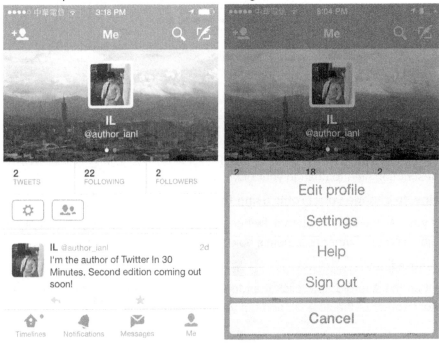

Navigating the Twitter interface

Once you have registered for Twitter, you may wonder how to navigate the service, and how to use certain features. This section will help you get your bearings, and explain what all of the icons, links, and buttons are for.

The Twitter icons explained

Twitter.com and the Twitter app for the iPhone and iPad use a set of icons to perform common functions. The Android app uses a slightly different set of icons.

On *twitter.com*, the Twitter toolbar runs across the top of the browser window:

Here is a brief description of the icons, from left to right:

- **Home**: The icon looks like a tiny house, and takes you to the home timeline view.

- **Notifications**: Click on the bell to see recent interactions with your Twitter account, such as someone following you, mentioning your Twitter account, or retweeting one of your tweets.

- **Discover**: The Discover icon is a pound symbol, known as a hashtag in Twitter parlance. It provides a tailored view of Twitter, generated by computer algorithms and an analysis of your activity on Twitter. The goals are to help you discover and respond to interesting tweets, as well as encourage you to follow other accounts. However, don't expect to find much in the way of obscure accounts or local tweets — I've found that the activity here often displays trending news and celebrity accounts.

- **Me**: The icon looks like the outline of a person's head and shoulders. Clicking it will display your public profile and personal timeline.

- **Search box**: Lets you search for words or phrases mentioned on Twitter, as well as accounts belonging to specific people and organizations. On the Twitter mobile app, tap the icon that looks like a magnifying glass.

- **Direct messages**: The icon that looks like an envelope shows a list of private messages between you and mutual followers.

- **Settings**: The gear icon lets you access security settings, change your password, update your profile, and log out of Twitter.

- **Compose new tweet**: The icon looks kind of like a quill on top of a piece of paper. Tapping it lets you write a new tweet.

These features are explained in more detail later in the guide.

Your home timeline

The first time you go to *twitter.com* and log in with your account credentials, you'll see a page containing your basic profile as well as a list of recent tweets created by other people. Here's what it looks like for me, logged in as @author_ianl:

This is my *home timeline*. At this point, I follow a limited number of famous Twitter accounts, so my home timeline is filled with tweets from TV personalities and major news outlets. Over time, this view will change as I start to follow friends, colleagues, local people, and other accounts that interest me. Later in this guide, I outline an approach for selecting Twitter accounts to follow, which will make for a more rewarding experience.

If you are using a mobile device, the Twitter app opens to your home timeline. You can also press the Home icon to see the home timeline.

Your personal timeline

Every Twitter account has its own timeline, which shows a list of recent tweets created by the account's owner. Earlier in this guide, we saw snapshots of the timelines belonging to @Oprah, @Momogoose, and

@RobertFischer. You can see practically any timeline by clicking on that person's or organization's Twitter handle. Profile information appears first, but if you scroll down the entire timeline will gradually become visible.

You can also view your own personal timeline. On *twitter.com*, click on the Me icon at the top of the screen. Here's what I see if press the Me icon or type http://twitter.com/author_ianl into the browser's address bar:

If you are using the Twitter app on an iPhone, iPad, or iPod touch, tap the Me icon to see your own timeline. If you are using an Android device, tap the More icon (which looks like three dots) and then select your Twitter handle.

CHAPTER THREE

Finding and following people on Twitter

Now that you have activated your Twitter account, you can start tweeting right away. (This is explained in more detail in the next chapter). First, however, we're going to cover the art of finding and following interesting accounts. Doing so will boost your Twitter experience in several important ways:

- The more people you follow, the more likely you are to see interesting things that you can share, explore, or respond to.

- Some people you follow on Twitter will follow you back, which can help build your Twitter network and increase the likelihood of your tweets being seen and responded to.

How to follow someone on Twitter

So you've signed up for Twitter, reserved your Twitter handle, set up a profile, and are ready to seize Twitter by the beak. This requires tweeting (described in Chapter 4), but you also want to see what other people are tweeting about and sharing on Twitter.

To see other people's tweets, you'll need to start following people. If you don't, Twitter will seem empty and boring, and you will quickly lose interest.

As described earlier in this guide, Twitter encourages new users to follow celebrity accounts. Twitter also urges users to upload their address books, and will try to match the email addresses of friends and other contacts with existing Twitter accounts.

But what if you want to follow a Twitter account after you have registered? The following sections explain how.

Follow an account online

Once you are registered for Twitter and have logged in, clicking on another person's Twitter handle will reveal that person's Twitter profile. Each profile contains a *Follow* button. Click it to follow the account. Once you do that,

that person's tweets will start appearing in your home timeline.

Below is an example of @JimmyFallon, the Twitter profile of television host and comedian Jimmy Fallon. You can visit his profile by typing *twitter.com/JimmyFallon* into the address bar of your browser. The *Follow* button is located below the description:

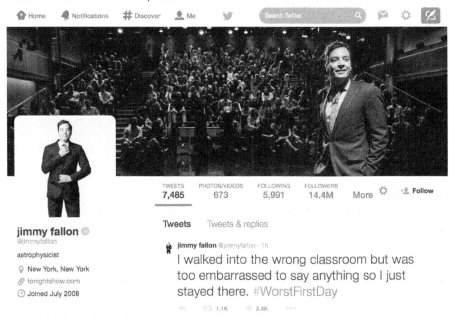

If you click the button, all the recent tweets created by @JimmyFallon will start showing up in your home timeline. Your home timeline consists of tweets from the Twitter accounts that you follow. The more accounts you follow, the more tweets you will see in your timeline.

Follow an account using the Twitter app

If you are using the Twitter app on your mobile device, tapping the handle of a Twitter user will reveal his or her profile. Click the *Follow* button to start following them: For the following Twitter user, the Android view is on the left and the iOS view is on the right:

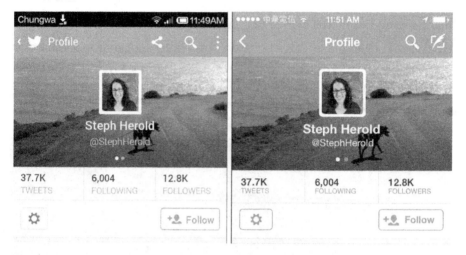

Alternately, you can use the Twitter app's search feature to find specific accounts to follow:

1. At the top of the screen, you will see an icon that looks like a magnifying glass. Tap it to open the search feature.

2. In the field provided, type the account name of the person or organization you want to follow.

3. The names of likely accounts will start to automatically populate the search field.

4. Once you have found the right account, click the *Follow* button.

Who should you follow?

Twitter has many mechanisms to help users find people to follow. If you've registered for Twitter (Chapter 2), you've already seen how Twitter suggests accounts belonging to famous people or organizations. Twitter can also leverage your address book list to identify friends and coworkers who are already on Twitter. The Discover icon provides a list of accounts tweeting about trending news and other events.

However, the sheer number of accounts and topics being discussed can be confusing to novice users. What's the best approach for deciding who to follow?

For a rewarding Twitter experience, it's crucial to identify accounts that are close to your own connections and interests. They might be friends, family members or colleagues. They could be people living in your town or city, or people from a location that's close to your heart — the place where you grew up, a favorite vacation spot, or a city or country you would like to visit.

I also advise new Twitter users to follow people who have shared causes or hobbies. Identify the experts or people with the best insights. Seek out sources of information that lead the conversation, such as a well-known publication, pundit, or thought leader. They don't have to be celebrities. In fact, many of the examples that follow are almost unknown outside of their areas of expertise.

Experts and leaders

Do you like political news? Are you the kind of person who feels a tingle of excitement when there's a scandal brewing, or do you like to follow wonky policy debates? Then follow @Politico, which is the Twitter account for the popular Washington-based news site of the same name. Political junkies may also want to follow the accounts of certain reporters, pundits and politicians.

Maybe you are a knitting fanatic. If that's the case, then @KnittingDaily is a good account to follow. People in this community share tips and new designs. There are even indie knitting rebels at @YarnHarlot.

Basketball freaks have their own Twitter buzz. This is due in large part to the active participation by professional and college players, as well as their fans. I recommend @SLAMonline or @ESPNNBA, as well as the account of player DeMarcus Cousins (@boogiecousins).

The disability community has developed a strident voice on Twitter. People with spinal cord injuries, low-vision users, and patients with other health conditions share their views of the world. There are advocacy efforts promoted by disability rights activists and family members. The accounts operated by Paralympic gold medallist @JessicaLong and @AAPD are good places to start.

At the start of this guide, I described the account of @JamesBondTheDog. **What if you're a cat person**? Twitter has you covered! One of the most popular Twitter cats is @sockington ("I am Jason Scott's cat"), with more than 1 million followers on Twitter. And then there's @RealGrumpyCat:

You get the idea. **Practically every interest, hobby, cause, and condition is represented on Twitter**. Sometimes it takes a little digging to find relevant and interesting accounts (more on that below), but once you follow them, you will feel connected to a group of kindred souls (or cats).

How to find specific accounts to follow

So you have an idea of who you want to follow. The next step is actually locating the accounts on Twitter.

It's not as easy as it sounds. While some people have obvious account names (such as @Oprah) others choose unusual Twitter handles. For instance, Ashton Kutcher uses @aplusk.

While many ordinary people use handles based on their actual names, it may not be clear which account should be followed if there are other Twitter users with similar names and handles.

However, there are ways of cutting through the confusion.

Twitter search

Twitter's search engine is a useful way to find accounts to follow. On the Twitter mobile app, tap the magnifying glass to open the search window. On *twitter.com*, the search window is located at the top of the page. Just start typing in names, and people's accounts will automatically begin to show up:

This is a great way to find accounts. I've been able to track down the Twitter accounts of musicians, businesspeople, authors, and old friends in this manner. However, Twitter search has limitations:

- Some people use Twitter without revealing their real names in their profiles. If you search for their names, you may not be able to find them.
- People with common names can be difficult to find on Twitter.

Here's an example that helps illustrate the problem. Let's say I wanted to find Bill Lee, the quirky Red Sox pitching ace from the 1970s known as "Spaceman" to his many fans. Typing "Bill Lee" into Twitter's search engine brings back a list of other men and women named Bill Lee, William Lee, or Billie Lee, but not my childhood baseball hero. However, by changing the search terms to "Spaceman Bill Lee," he shows up:

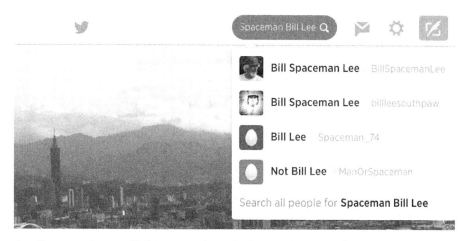

Another way to use Twitter search to find accounts is to search for words or phrases that people might use in a tweet. Let's say you wanted to find other people who like Oprah's Book Club. Searching for that phrase brings up some interesting results, ranging from a link to the official Oprah's Book Club account on Twitter to random tweets by readers:

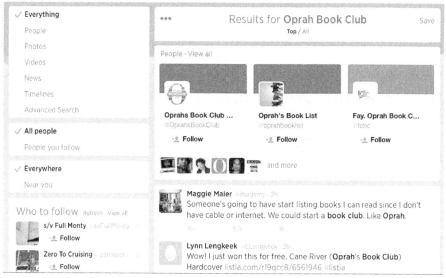

You can use the same technique to search for local accounts. For instance, if you like Chicago basketball, search for "Chicago Bulls" or the name of a Bulls player. If you are interested in politics in San Diego, search for "San

Diego politics" or the name of the mayor.

By default, Twitter shows Top Tweets in the list of results presented on the screen. Top Tweets have either been created by people with an extensive Twitter presence, or the tweets have been widely shared on Twitter. Be sure to click the *All* link in the results page to see the posts by everyone else, which may be more interesting or detailed than the Top Tweets!

How to find friends on Twitter

Twitter is used by hundreds of millions of people, so there is a good chance that at least a few people you know have active Twitter accounts. You may have encountered them when you registered your account, if you used the option that lets Twitter scan your contact lists.

There are other ways to find friends on Twitter. In addition to Twitter's search engine, The easiest way to do it is to ask ... on Facebook! Here's what you can post on Facebook:

> *"Friends, I am building up my Twitter network at @bobsmith102. Please follow me or your leave your Twitter handle in the comments to this Facebook post."*

You can also search for people's Twitter handles on Google. Just type a name and "twitter" and see what turns up. Note, however, that this method will not identify people who used an alias or initials when they registered for Twitter.

How to find local accounts to follow

The great thing about tapping into local accounts in Twitter is that it allows you to gain new insights into your community and the people who live there.

Here are common starting points:

Local media: You may already get the local paper delivered to your house, or tune into the local TV news from time to time. I have found that Twitter accounts operated by local media sometimes have extra goodies, including live reports from local events or details that get left out of the 10 o'clock news.

To start following a media account, you'll have to find the Twitter profile first. If it can't be found in Twitter's search engine, go to the online presence of the news organization. The home page will often have a little blurb that says "Follow us on Twitter!" with either a link to the Twitter profile or the account name preceded by the @ symbol.

For instance, my local paper's Twitter account is @NewtonTab. To go to the Twitter profile, I just type *twitter.com/newtontab* in the address bar of the browser.

Besides links to online news stories or breaking police and fire incidents, additional information gets shared. Here's one update from my local paper, talking about a local baseball game:

The reporter who wrote it let his followers know that the game can be watched on NESN, a sports cable channel serving New England. This is information I can use!

Besides following the account of the paper or individual reporters, you can also use local media accounts to find other local people or institutions to follow. For instance, my local paper sometimes retweets messages from our mayor, Setti Warren (@MayorWarren). Clicking his Twitter handle brings up his profile:

From there, all I need to do is press the Follow button, and I'll be able to see the mayor's tweets in my timeline.

Local bloggers: Somewhere in your community, someone is writing a blog. Blog authors are people who feel compelled to write about topics that are important to them. It could be about their lives, their hobbies or interests, their children, their areas of expertise, or even uncomfortable topics such as living with disease or divorce.

You may not know who these people are. Indeed, they may not want you to know who they are, but they are there, and they love to write. They often love to tweet, too.

To find local bloggers who write about local issues, Google "blog" and the name of your town or community. Check out the blogs that are highlighted, and look for a Twitter symbol on the front page. Click the symbol to be taken to the blogger's Twitter account. If you like what you see, follow the account!

Local businesses and organizations: In Chapter 1, I used the example of the @momogoose food truck, which uses Twitter to stay connected with its customers. Many other local businesses also use Twitter. The next time you visit a local coffee shop, clothes boutique, restaurant or library, look around for a "Follow us on Twitter!" sign. These days, savvy businesses use Twitter to connect with local patrons who want to learn about incoming products, special deals, new branches, or other insights.

You don't need to visit the building in person to find out if a business has a Twitter account. Google the company online, and see if the company's website contains a link to a Twitter account.

Random local people: Once you've identified local media, bloggers and businesses, and are following them on Twitter, check out the *Following* and *Followers* links on their profile pages. You're sure to find local people in the lists. For instance, in my local newspaper's list of followers, I found these Twitter accounts:

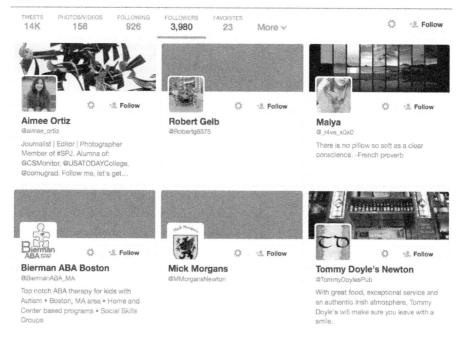

TWEETS	PHOTOS/VIDEOS	FOLLOWING	FOLLOWERS	FAVORITES		
14K	156	926	**3,980**	23	More v	Follow

Aimee Ortiz
@aimee_ortiz
Journalist | Editor | Photographer Member of #SPJ. Alumna of: @CSMonitor, @USATODAYCollege, @cornugrad. Follow me, let's get...

Robert Gelb
@Robertg8375

Maiya
@_r4ve_x0x0
There is no pillow so soft as a clear conscience. -French proverb

Bierman ABA Boston
@BiermanABA_MA
Top notch ABA therapy for kids with Autism • Boston, MA area • Home and Center based programs • Social Skills Groups

Mick Morgans
@MMorgansNewton

Tommy Doyle's Newton
@TommyDoylesPub
With great food, exceptional service and an authentic Irish atmosphere, Tommy Doyle's will make sure you leave with a smile.

Clicking through to the profiles, I was able to identify people in my community. How? Sometimes people include their hometowns on their Twitter profiles, or they may reference people, places, or issues in their tweets which give clues to where they are located.

You can do the same thing, starting with local media and businesses and trying to identify local followers. You may not know these people, and they may not use their real names on Twitter. Nevertheless, it's OK to follow them.

They may even follow you back!

Twitter's recommendation algorithm

If you are using Twitter on the Web, you'll notice a list of recommended accounts when you go to your home page at *twitter.com*. They are listed under the *Who To Follow* box, which appears on the right side of the page:

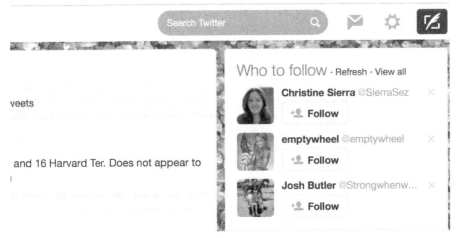

Twitter uses algorithms and behavioral data to generate the recommendations. From time to time, interesting accounts will show up, and they can be immediately followed. However, if you're a new user, there may not be enough behavioral data to generate recommendations. As a result, the *Who To Follow* box will probably show lots of celebrities as well as Promoted Accounts, which usually belong to brands advertising on Twitter.

How many accounts should a new user follow?

How many people and organizations should you follow on Twitter? That's up to you. I have seen people who follow tens of thousands of other Twitter accounts. While they never have a shortage of tweets to read, I question the value of the information they are getting in their home timelines — the most interesting or relevant information tends to be lost in the fire hose of tweets.

A better strategy, at least in the beginning, is to follow a limited number of people or organizations that are more likely to maintain your interest and engage with you. Once you've gotten the hang of Twitter, grow the list as slowly or as quickly as you like.

Following 50 other Twitter accounts is a good starting point. It doesn't take that long to follow 50 accounts, and if you pick wisely, you'll start getting value from your list right away.

Protected accounts

A small number of Twitter accounts are partially closed off to public view. The profile picture, total numbers of followers, and other information are shown. However, the owner's tweets, the identities of followers, and the accounts he or she is following are hidden. A small lock icon on the profile indicates that the account is *protected*.

Why would someone set up a protected Twitter account, or switch his or her account from open to protected status? Here are some reasons:

- The owner does not want to share his or her tweets for personal reasons, or because of a desire for privacy.

- Certain people, such as a celebrity embroiled in a scandal, may want to temporarily avoid scrutiny. He or she will re-open the account once the hubbub dies down.

- People or organizations want to reserve a Twitter handle so no one else grabs it, but the owner is not ready to start tweeting.

It's possible to follow a protected account. However, you will first need to be approved by the owner. Simply click the *Follow* button, and a notification will be sent to the owner of the account. He or she can then approve or reject the request. If you are approved, you will be able to see his or her tweets.

If you get rejected, don't take it hard. There are many other interesting accounts to follow, as we'll see later this chapter.

Accounts to avoid

Before I follow anyone in Twitter, I check their tweets. If they don't tweet often, or the tweets are boring (for instance, just links to news stories) I won't follow them. Here are some other red flags:

Egg accounts. Egg accounts are often new or abandoned accounts, created by people who haven't uploaded a profile picture to Twitter. For people who have just started tweeting, an egg account is normal (maybe you're an egg, too!). However, egg accounts which haven't been updated in months or years are not worth following. The people who own them have given up on Twitter, and most likely won't ever share something of interest.

Rude birds. Some people on Twitter use Twitter to belittle others, spread bizarre observations, or share intimate details of their warped lives. The tweets are littered with swears and stupidity. Sometimes the accounts belong to teens who don't know any better. Sometimes they belong to adults who haven't matured. Rarely do they offer insights or information of value. Don't bother following them.

Spam accounts. Not long after you start using Twitter, you will receive a notification that someone is following you. Most of the time, the followers are legitimate — maybe they are people you know, or people who are following you because of some shared interest.

But others may look a little...off. The tweets seem vapid or unauthentic. They follow hundreds or thousands of people, but have very few people following them back. Links appear in their feeds that don't come from well-known domains. In addition, the profile pictures tend to show unusually attractive people. Here's an example:

football game was awesome let's relax now

Don't get your hopes up if someone like this follows you. Random attractive people probably don't want to follow you (or me, for that matter). In fact, such accounts do not belong to attractive strangers tweeting about football, travel, and hooking up. These accounts actually belong to spammers, and my guess is most of them are unattractive, basement-dwelling losers who tweet links to low-grade dating sites, advertisements or online shopping portals that might generate a few pennies every time someone clicks. Don't click the links, and don't follow them back!

How to unfollow a Twitter account

Here's the situation: You're following @Oprah, but the relentless promotion of her media empire on Twitter is driving you nuts. It's gotten to the point that when Oprah's profile picture pops up in your Twitter feed, you involuntarily groan in anticipation of another self-congratulatory tweet about a free car giveaway or her new television program. Please, make it stop!

The easy way to unfollow anyone on Twitter is to simply click the *Unfollow* button on his or her profile. For instance, to ditch Oprah on the Twitter website, you would go to @Oprah's online Twitter profile (*twitter.com/oprah*). The *Following* button confirms you are following her, but if you hover your mouse over the button, it turns into an *Unfollow* button:

Once you have unfollowed @Oprah, her tweets will no longer be automatically fed into your home timeline. Huzzah!

How to quickly unfollow lots of people

If you want to unfollow lots of people at once, there is an easy way to do it. Go to your own profile and select *Following*. Doing so brings up a list of all of the Twitter accounts you are following. Hover over one of the buttons, and it turns to an *Unfollow* button:

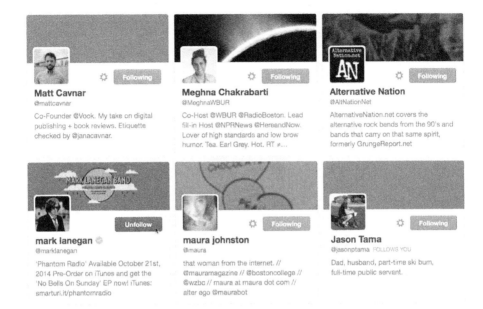

Press it to unfollow the account, and then repeat for any other accounts that no longer interest you.

On the mobile app, here are the steps to unfollow accounts:

1. Open the Twitter app, and go to your own Twitter profile.

2. Press *Following*.

3. You will see a list of accounts that you are currently following, with a small button with a checkmark next to each profile. Press the button next to each account you want to unfollow.

Help! I'm being followed

What happens when someone follows you on Twitter? This is the message that you will see in your email inbox:

In 30 Minutes Guides,
You have a new follower on Twitter.

Tom Litchfield
@tomlitchfield

Yup, I'm a CEO too. Wordpress expert, can fix almost anything online for biz,
#Nonprofits and NGOs. #apps #gadgets #animals #vegetarian #cleantech
#SFGiants
SF Bay Area

Followed by Mark Harai and 12 others.
Following: 31839 · Followers: 34311

 Follow

You can also see a list of all of your followers. Go to your profile page on Twitter and click the *Followers* link. All of the accounts following you will be presented in reverse-chronological order.

It may seem strange that these people are following your tweets. Who are they? How did they find out about you? What are their intentions?

For most accounts, it's easy to figure out who they are: Just click on the link to see their profile page and the recent tweets they've made.

As for how they found out about you, and why they are following you, those are harder questions to answer. In many cases, they may have stumbled upon you by using Twitter's search engine or looking at someone else's list of followers (for instance, if you follow @Oprah or the local newspaper, you will show up on those two accounts' lists of followers). They may think your tweets are funny or insightful, or you share some common interest.

Most of the time, it's harmless attention. These strangers will see your tweets, and may even start a dialogue at some point.

But "following" is not synonymous with "stalking." Twitter creates value by sharing information and letting people and organizations expand their networks, even with strangers who they may never meet in person.

Remember also that anyone can see your tweets. All they need to do is load your profile into their web browsers. Even if they aren't following you, they will still see your tweets.

In other words, your tweets are public information. If you don't want anyone to see them, then you should protect your tweets…or not use Twitter at all.

Information on how to block specific users from following you and how to protect your tweets is described below.

How to block certain followers

If someone starts following you and you don't want them to, you can block them. Here's how to do it online:

1. Go to *twitter.com* and click the *Followers* links.

2. The page will display a list of accounts following you. Find the account you want to block.

3. Next to the *Follow* button is a gear icon. Click it, and select *Block* or *Report*.

4. A pop-up menu will appear. Select the option that most applies:

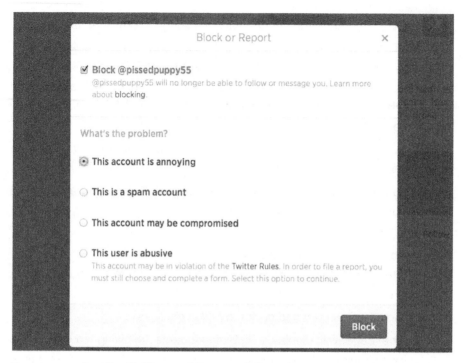

If you are using the Twitter mobile app, follow these steps to block another user:

1. Open the app and go your profile by pressing the Me or More icon.

2. Tap *Followers*.

3. Find the account you want to block and tap the name.

4. Tap the gear icon and select *Block* or *Report*.

How to protect an account

If you don't want your tweets to be seen by the world, or you want more control over who follows you, you can use a Twitter feature called Protect My Tweets. It basically locks down the account so no one except your followers can see what you are tweeting.

If you are new to Twitter, protecting your account will make it very difficult to start conversations and gain followers. However, if you have a pressing reason to close your tweets to public view, follow these steps:

1. Go to *twitter.com* and log on.

2. Click the gear icon and select *Settings.*

3. Select the menu titled *Security And Privacy.*

4. Under Privacy, select the *Protect My Tweets* option:

When you are done, click the *Save Change* button at the bottom of the page.

CHAPTER FOUR

Tweeting

You've created an account, and are now following other people on Twitter. Now it's time to start tweeting! This chapter explains how to send tweets, participate in discussions, and start discussions of your own.

How to create a tweet

Creating a new tweet is a cinch, and Twitter gives you multiple ways to do it.

Online:

Go to *twitter.com* and make sure you are logged in. Look for the *Compose* field on the left side of the page:

1. Place your cursor in the field, and start typing.

2. As you type, a counter below the field counts down how many characters you have left. Once you have typed 140 characters, the number will turn negative, meaning the tweet will be truncated to 140 characters unless you manually reduce the overage.

3. When you are ready to release your tweet to the world, click the *Tweet* button.

There's another way to compose a new tweet from your profile page. In the upper right corner of the page, next to the Settings button, is a rectangular button overlaid with a feather-like icon. Click it to write a new tweet.

Twitter app:

Twitter's mobile apps are also easy to use, although they will require you to use a smaller keyboard.

1. On Apple devices, find the Compose icon, which looks like a small rectangle with a feather lying across it. On Android, look for the *What's happening* prompt at the bottom of the home screen.

2. Use the keyboard or the dictation function on your device to create the tweet.

3. Tap the *Tweet* button when you are ready to send it.

Deciding what to tweet about

While creating a tweet is easy, deciding what to tweet about can be tricky for newcomers.

Keep in mind that writing great tweets will involve understanding your audience and seeing what works for them, while keeping true to your own style of communication. Sometimes it's helpful to look to other people for inspiration, but as I explain later in this section, the tone of the conversation can change depending on who you follow. I also discuss how to get past mental blocks associated with using this new medium for the first time.

Finally, I have some practical tips about how to come up with great tweets to get the ball rolling.

What do other people usually tweet about?

What kinds of things do people tweet about in their 140-character messages? It really depends on who you follow. In Chapter 1, I showed you some individual examples of tweets by a famous person (@Oprah), a small business (@Momogoose) and several ordinary users. But if you follow hundreds of people, chances are you will see some patterns emerge, based on their interests.

For instance, if I were to use a phrase to describe the tweets from the hundreds of people I follow (a mix of journalists, tech/Web people, people from the Boston area and random friends), it would be "observations about life, careers, and major events, with lots of overlap."

Here's another way to break it down:

Observations: People have interests, activities, and professional backgrounds, which will be reflected in their tweets. Someone has just finished a book, cooked a meal, attended a meeting, gone for a jog, or commented on the weather.

Major events: When there's a major event, such as a natural disaster, political scandal or a splashy gadget release, a surge of topical tweets occurs as people I know react to or *retweet* the news (more about retweeting later in this guide). For instance, the night Apple founder Steve Jobs died, about half of the people I followed had something to say about it. National elections and the Olympics also bring out a lot of Twitter commentary.

Overlap: On any given weekend, many of the people I follow will be watching the same TV show or sporting event. Because I follow so many technology people, I see a lot of references to companies such as Google, Apple, and Microsoft.

But here's the thing: What I see on Twitter is not representative of what other people see. A fashionista in Manhattan will have a far different experience with Twitter, based on her interests and the people she follows. She will see more tweets and photos involving clothing, shoes, accessories, and sales, as well as more information specific to New York City.

A football fan in Florida is more likely to follow other football fans whose tweets include football references. A programmer living in Paris is more likely to see tweets about programming and his or her neighborhood in the 19th arrondissement. What about a housewife in Hollywood? Or a scientist in Singapore? They will follow different types of people, and will see and send different types of tweets.

Of course, you can follow the lead of other accounts and start tweeting about similar topics. But it's also possible to develop your own voice, as I describe below.

Mental blocks to tweeting

A lot of people feel strange using Twitter for the first time. "Why would anyone care about what I have to say?" is one comment I constantly hear from new users. Others feel slightly uncomfortable sharing information publicly, even if the information is not particularly sensitive or important. A few people complain that they don't have enough room to say what they want to say in just 140 characters.

Here are some responses to put your mind at ease:

"The stuff I have to say is too boring." Most people won't be particularly interested in the fact that your cat Mr. Elmer P. McFurrikins is curled up on the couch right now, and boy, doesn't he look cute?

But tweets about the mundane aspects of your life contain something that is vitally important to gaining followers and taking part in discussions: *authenticity*.

Tweets about the weather, the crowds at the mall, your kid's basketball game, and even your cat demonstrate that you are a real person, are probably friendly, and are willing to share information about your life.

Considering the number of cat people in the world, I wouldn't be surprised if you got a response like this:

"140 characters isn't enough to say what I want to say!"

I used to be like this. As a blogger accustomed to writing hundreds of words at a time, the idea of short bursts on Twitter seemed limiting. But I quickly learned that it's possible to say quite a bit in 140 characters. Observations can be brief, identifying key pieces of information:

Opinions don't have to be long, either, as in this tweet about a recent basketball game:

When deep analysis or description is required, that's when posting photographs and links to long-form material comes in handy.

Lastly, Twitter teaches you to be spare with words. The character counter can inform you if a tweet is too long:

The tweet, which was nearly twice as long as Twitter allows, was eventually reduced to a compact version that has 13 characters to spare:

"I'm uncomfortable sharing information publicly." The idea of posting opinions, observations and other snippets of life for others (including complete strangers) to see can be a little unnerving at first.

For some people, it's an unfamiliar concept. For others, there is a worry about tweeting something that might put them in a bad light. And then there are those who like the idea of tweeting, but get concerned that certain people might spot a specific tweet ("What will my boss/neighbor/ex-boyfriend think if they see the tweet I made on Saturday night?").

Finding your comfort level

With Twitter, keep in mind that *you don't have to share any more information than you want to share*. Here are tips for dialing things down to keep them at a level that makes you comfortable:

- Your Twitter handle does not have to reflect your actual name. If @bobcsmith22 is too revealing, use @bobbiec22 or @McTurtleman.

- You can remove elements from your Twitter profile, or substitute more anonymous information. You don't have to use a real name in your profile. You can leave your location blank, and use a photo of your cat or dog instead of a real profile photo.

- To reduce the chance of certain people seeing your tweets, avoid mentioning their names (which can appear in search engine results) or Twitter handles (which show up in their Notifications area) when you are tweeting.

- If you are about to tweet something that might be considered controversial or offensive, take some time to reflect on the contents of the tweet before posting it for others to see.

Controversial and angry tweets

On this last point, you can also use softer language. For instance, after seeing dog doo in the local park, you might be inclined to fire off an angry tweet:

That's liable to rub *all* dog owners the wrong way. How about tweeting something that not only clarifies who is at fault, but also starts a constructive dialogue?

One final comment regarding controversial tweets: Check your employer's online communications policies before tweeting information or photos that relate to your job. Many companies have guidelines that cover social media use by their employees.

Tips for writing great tweets

So you've gotten over your hang-ups about tweeting. Here's where the rubber hits the road — it's time to start tweeting! But what can you tweet about?

The obvious answer is "anything you feel comfortable sharing." I'm going to make it a little easier for you by suggesting a few ways to get those creative juices flowing.

Tip #1: What did you see/hear/experience in the last 24 hours that was notable?

It could have been a memorable play in last night's football game, the Chinese food you ate for lunch, the classic song you're listening to now, or the clothes people are wearing on the street:

Emily Ramsey
@EmilyLRamsey

A lot of weather confused dressing in London today. I've seen long boots, flip flops, fur coats and denim shorts. Make your mind up London

↩ Reply ♺ Retweet ★ Favorite ••• More

12:56 AM - 13 Aug 2014

Tip #2: What made you laugh out loud?

Humor is all around you. Colleagues, neighbors, children, and strangers will sometimes say or do something that makes you laugh. TV shows and other mass media are another source of laughter. These moments can be shared on Twitter. And, of course, one-liners are made for Twitter.

Tip #3: What tidbit would you share with friends, coworkers, or neighbors?

What sorts of information do you share in the real world? Do you have any personal updates or observations that could be shared publicly? It's a bad idea to share malicious or embarrassing gossip ("Did you see how plastered Dave was at the barbecue?"). However, other bits of neighborly news that you or other people might say aloud can be shared on Twitter:

Tip #4: What would you say on Facebook?

In many cases, information or observations you share on Facebook can be pasted directly into Twitter afterward. There are even Twitter applications that allow people to post to Facebook and Twitter simultaneously, without copying and pasting. On the official companion website for this guide (located at *twitter.in30minutes.com*) I have included a review of one such application called Hootsuite.

Of course, do not tweet information that's meant to stay in a closed conversation on Facebook. Remember, almost all tweets are public, whereas most Facebook posts are intended to be limited to a small group of people.

Tip #5: Share an interesting link

Sharing links on Twitter is a great way to spread news, videos, shopping deals, or useful online resources. It's easy to do, and Twitter automatically substitutes a shortened link to help keep your tweets below the 140-character limit.

The easy way to share a link:

You may notice that many articles, blogs, YouTube videos and websites have icons, buttons, and links to make tweeting easier:

Yet Another Flight Diverted After Battle Over Reclining Seats

Andy Cush
Filed to: UNFRIENDLY SKIES   Yesterday 9:38am

40,195 🔥 3 ★ ▼

Share to Kinja

Share to Facebook

Share to Twitter

Go to permalink

If you click the button or link, it will allow you to share the headline and the link on Twitter. Regardless of whether you are on a desktop computer or smartphone, you may be prompted to log into Twitter to allow sharing of the link with your followers.

You may also be able to edit the tweet before it goes out, but don't edit or delete the link itself. Press Submit to share the link.

The hard way to share a link:

You will need two browsers open at the same time, or two browser tabs:

1. Open up one browser and load *twitter.com*. The other browser should have the news story, video or Web page displayed, along with the URL in the address bar.

2. Copy the headline (right-click with your mouse and select *Copy*).

3. Switch to the browser with Twitter, and paste the headline into the area where you compose a tweet (right-click and select *Paste*). Or type a summary or your opinion ("Must-read article about the Flying Burrito Brothers").

4. Go back to the browser window with the interesting webpage. Go to the address bar and copy the entire URL.

5. Switch to the browser with Twitter, and paste the URL after the

headline or text you've written.

6. Make sure there is a space between the text and the headline in your tweet.

7. Don't worry if the tweet is too long — Twitter will substitute a short link.

8. Press the *Send* button.

Tip #6: Ask other people for help

Twitter is a great place to ask for advice. I'm not talking about serious, soul-searching questions ("Should I marry him?") but rather the quick questions that your followers or other Twitter denizens may be able to help with. For instance:

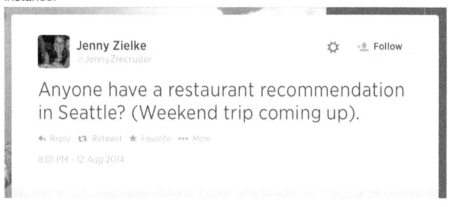

Jenny Zielke
@JennyZrecruiter

Follow

Anyone have a restaurant recommendation in Seattle? (Weekend trip coming up).

↩ Reply ↻ Retweet ★ Favorite ••• More

8:01 PM - 12 Aug 2014

Tips for taking great photos

Photos are a great way to connect with followers. They're easy to post, too.

When you write a tweet on *twitter.com* (left) or using the Twitter mobile app (right), you'll notice a camera or photo icon below the text field:

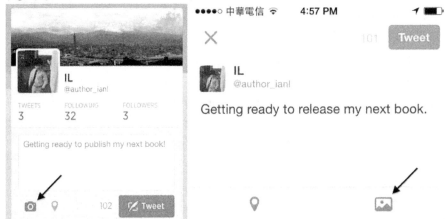

Clicking or tapping the icon allows you to choose a photo to include in your tweet. The photo may already exist on your hard drive or mobile phone, or you can create a new one. Twitter will upload the photo to its servers when you post the tweet. The photo will be automatically displayed to those followers using *twitter.com* or the Twitter mobile app.

As you might expect, people like to share photos of interesting or beautiful sights, as well as food, pets and family vacations. But I've also seen people using photos to illustrate a situation, such as a car with an unusual license plate:

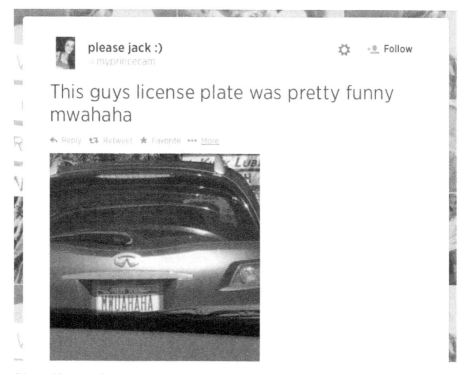

(Note: Never take a picture or attempt to tweet while you are driving!)

Unexpected or uncommon scenes tend to get noticed. Recently, I was on a flight that was aborted not long after takeoff. The pilot announced the Boeing 747 would be dumping all of its fuel before returning to the airport. Here's the photo I took and tweeted:

What photos should you share on Twitter? It depends on what you think is interesting...or what you think your audience will like. Try a few shots, and see how people react!

How to delete tweets

So you've created a tweet. What if you want to get rid of it?

On the Web:

1. Go to *twitter.com* and click on your name, or on the link that shows the total number of tweets you've made. This will bring up a list of all of your tweets, with the newest tweets at the top of the list.

2. Find the tweet you want to delete. Look for the tiny trashcan icon (see image) and click it.

3. You will be asked to confirm the deletion one last time. Once you give your approval, the tweet is gone!

Phone or tablet:

1. Open your Twitter application.

2. Tap the Profile icon, which will show a list of your recent tweets (to see older tweets, click the *Tweets* link that shows the number of total tweets beside it).

3. Find the tweet you want to delete in the list of tweets, and tap it.

4. The tweet will appear alone on the screen. Tap the icon that looks like a trash can to delete it. If you don't see it, tap the More icon (three dots) and then select *Delete*.

5. You will be asked to confirm whether you want to delete it. Select *Yes*.

The tweet will be removed from your stream.

Regardless of which method you use to delete a specific tweet, it may still live on if someone else has retweeted it or it's been manually saved by other people.

CHAPTER FIVE

Advanced Twitter: Joining the discussion

Twitter is not just about one-way tweets. It's possible to have conversations on Twitter with other people, and connect and share in other ways. We'll explore Twitter discussions in the following pages.

In addition, many Twitter users employ unfamiliar conventions, such as the letters "RT" and hashtags. Once you understand how the syntax works, you'll realize Twitter discussions mirror the ways in which humans have always talked and shared information.

We'll also examine how a single tweet can reach thousands or even millions of people in a short period of time. Tweets that "go viral" can be incredibly informative, but can also spread incorrect information.

Someone responded to my tweet!

One day, in your Notifications area (look for the bell icon), you may see a response to one of your earlier tweets. Here's an example:

You can create an "@reply" (pronounced "at-reply") by clicking the *Reply* link below a tweet. Try it on any tweet in your home timeline. You'll see that Twitter automatically starts the reply with the Twitter handle of the person you are responding to. Then it's up to you to add additional text, which might be a comment or more information. Click the *Tweet* button to send your @reply.

Note that @replies won't be seen by other users unless they too follow the account that starts the tweet, or they are actively looking at all of the tweets from a specific account. So, if by some miracle @Oprah sent an @reply to one of your tweets, none of your followers would see it, unless they too were following @Oprah.

Why don't famous people respond to my tweets?

After releasing the first edition of this book, I received an email from a user who was puzzled why well-known Twitter accounts never responded to his tweets.

It's a fair question. Twitter is a great way to connect with people, and it's so easy to respond to a tweet.

However, actors, musicians, politicians, TV stars, and well-known organizations and brands live by a different set of rules on Twitter. Here are some reasons high-profile accounts seldom respond:

- The tweets from fans are hard to understand ("Loved that thing you said the other night at your concert! #LOL").
- The tweets are insulting ("You look like a pregnant cow on TV").
- The tweets ask questions which are difficult to answer in 140 characters ("What are your thoughts about Tibetan Buddhism?").
- When it comes to controversial issues, famous accounts don't want to take sides or make statements that might harm their public stature.
- Celebrities don't have enough time to reply to everyone.

Regarding this last point, while it's easy to send out a single tweet to a single fan, the math doesn't work for large numbers of fans. For instance, even if @Oprah took a break from promoting the latest Oprah's Book Club selection and decided to say "Hi!" to each one of her Twitter followers every minute of every day, it would take over 17,000 years to get through the more than 25 million accounts currently following her.

Someone mentioned me!

When browsing your Notifications, you may notice tweets from other people that contain your Twitter handle, but are not responding to something you've tweeted about. Here's an example:

These are called @mentions (pronounced "at-mentions"). They often contain acknowledgements, questions, or some other piece of information that the person who created the tweet wants you to see.

For instance, every day scores of people @mention the Twitter handle of a Boston-based blog called Universal Hub, to ask a question, share a special photo, or draw the editor's attention to some piece of local news:

If you receive an @mention, it's up to you how to respond. In some cases, no response is necessary.

Unfortunately, spammers and malicious hackers have latched onto @mentions. They know that you will probably read a tweet that includes your Twitter handle. These spammers and hackers use @mentions to spread links to porn, coupon sites, and sites that install malware on visitors' computers. Be suspicious of click-bait that mentions your Twitter handle and includes a link to an unfamiliar website. If it's from an unknown Twitter account with a small number of previous tweets, it's probably spam.

Retweets

Retweet, v. to repeat someone else's tweet, while giving credit to the original author; n. A tweet that has been copied and rebroadcast on another Twitter account, with the capital letters "RT" and the Twitter handle of the original sender added to the front of the new tweet.

You've just read my definition of a *retweet*, but an example should make the concept clear:

What's going on here? The Twitter account @Inspire_Us tweeted an observation about life. Another account, @rosellatorres25, thought the message was noteworthy, and decided to repeat it using the letters "RT" (which means "retweet") and the original tweet.

Rosella probably did not type out the entire tweet. It's much easier to click the *Retweet* link below the original message, which automatically copies the handle of the author and the contents of the original tweet, and then posts it.

It's also important to note that @rosellatorres25 acknowledged the original author by including "RT" and the @Inspire_Us Twitter handle. If Rosella had simply copied the message, but failed to credit the source, that's not a retweet. It's just copying.

Why do people retweet other people's tweets? Often, it's for the same reason that people might repeat what they heard from a friend, coworker, or neighbor — it's information, news or a clever phrase that's worth repeating.

Some people, when RTing someone else, like to add a little comment before the RT symbol ("Agreed!" or "Read this"). Others may shorten the original tweet to ensure the extra characters don't push the retweet over 140 characters.

Hashtags explained

You may notice that some words in tweets have the hashtag symbol (#) added to the front. Occasionally, there will be a hashtagged phrase or acronym with all of the spaces and periods removed. Hashtags are sometimes seen on advertisements or in television programs.

Hashtags are a Twitter convention that lets people easily find tweets about a certain topic. By adding a hashtag to the front of a word or phrase, it turns it into a link that points to Twitter's search engine. Click the link, and the most recent tweets which include the same hashtag are displayed. For example, here's what shows up when I click on *#Bulls*:

The *#Bulls* hashtag lets me see tweets from other fans, as well as news from various blogs and sports reporters. It's a very convenient way to connect with other like-minded people.

Hashtags serve other useful functions as well. They alert other Twitter followers to the fact that the tweet is about a certain topic that may not otherwise be apparent. For instance, let's say you're watching the Oscars on TV, and you see someone wearing a beautiful dress glide by the camera. You could ask your Twitter followers:

But followers not watching the program may not know what you are talking about. However, they will figure it out if you add an appropriate hashtag:

By adding *#oscars*, it's clear you are talking about the awards ceremony, and not something else. Moreover, anyone clicking on the *#oscars* link online or on their Twitter app will see all of the other tweets with the *#oscars* hashtag.

Sometimes people create funny hashtags. The television host Jimmy Fallon and his writing team are especially skilled at this. They ask their viewing audience a funny question and then tell them to use a hashtag to let the writing team (and other viewers) see the answers. Here are some responses to his hashtag *#WorstCarlEverHad*:

Hashtags are also used to reference sporting events (*#olympics*), political races (*#election2016*), conferences (*#ces2015*), and many other types of events.

Practical uses for hashtags

Jimmy Fallon uses hashtags to communicate with his audience. Bulls fans use hashtags to discuss their favorite team. Other people use hashtags to draw attention to specific topics, or to associate their tweets with places, concepts, and more.

Hashtags have additional uses:

1. **Adding a hashtagged topic to a question can help generate answers**. For example, if I wanted to ask my followers about the best Cuban restaurant in Miami, adding *#Miami* or *#cubanfood* to the end of my tweet would generate some additional eyeballs from people who follow that topic, but don't follow me.

2. **Hashtags are a way to catch the attention of companies, event organizers, journalists, and other people who have a strong interest in a certain topic**. I once attended an event that had its

own hashtag, and used the hashtag in my tweets for an entire day. Later that day, I was introduced to the event organizer. He already knew who I was — he had been following the hashtag all day and had seen my tweets. Adding that hashtag to my tweets helped me make a stronger connection in the real world.

Hashtag no-nos

Some new Twitter users make the mistake of turning every word in their tweets into hashtags. Here's an example:

It's irritating, unnecessary, and hard to read. In addition, hashtagging common nouns, verbs and other words doesn't add any value or insights. Clicking *#up* or *#my* in Twitter will return a list of random tweets about all kinds of topics, rather than a focused list based on specific topics.

Another mistake: using the wrong hashtag. For instance, followers of the Boston Red Sox generally use *#redsox* to talk about their team, not *#bostonredsox* or *#sox*.

Mistakes can also happen when a single hashtag is used by two different groups of people. Check out *#gastro*, which is used by people who like gourmet food as well as doctors and scientists who are interested in discussing gastrointestinal diseases:

Bottom line: Choose your hashtags carefully. If I am interested in using a particular hashtag in a tweet, I often search Twitter first to make sure it's the appropriate one to use.

Going viral

Twitter discussions and retweets can sometimes lead to a piece of news, a photo, or some other piece of information "going viral." Here's what it looks like:

CIA @CIA · Jul 17

The camera could take photos after release or on a pre-set delay. Details of #pigeon missions are still classified.

1.5K   1.2K   • • •   View more photos and videos

This is a strange photo tweeted by the Central Intelligence Agency (yes, even spy agencies use Twitter) with a funny description that evokes images of spy pigeons flying over the Berlin Wall to carry out secret missions.

Below the photo, the circling arrows icon indicates that more than 1,500 other Twitter accounts have retweeted this photo, or shared it with their followers. It is very unusual for a single tweet to be shared so widely, but if the information or image is special, it can go viral.

How does a viral tweet spread? Let's say you post a cute picture of your cat playing the piano. Maybe two of your followers retweet this piece of information. What happens then are some followers of those two friends retweet it again, then each of the retweets are again retweeted by *their* followers, and so on...kind of like the old shampoo commercial!

If it gets retweeted enough, eventually a celebrity, politician, major news organization or some other widely followed or trusted source will retweet it, at which point thousands or even millions of people are retweeting the same piece of information in a short period of time.

When something goes viral, it can lead to more followers and publicity for the person who first tweeted the information.

But there is a dark side to going viral, too. What if the information is incorrect, someone tweets a hoax, or the piano-playing cat was photoshopped?

This is not a hypothetical situation. It's happened before, and not just with innocent pieces of information or funny cat photos. Let's say someone tweets a piece of juicy gossip. It snowballs, but later it turns out that the information was false. In extreme cases, people have had their deaths prematurely reported, or have been fingered for crimes they did not commit. By the time the truth comes out, reputations have been damaged. Oftentimes, the people who tweeted or retweeted the false information are very embarrassed.

Because of the potential for false information to spread virally through retweets, I advise people to be careful when retweeting details relating to crimes, disasters, scandals, or unconfirmed news items. People can be hurt when false rumors are retweeted. Check the news or some other reliable source first.

Advanced features

While we don't have enough time to cover all aspects of Twitter, there are a few additional features and tools you should be aware of. They include Direct Messages, Favorites, Lists, and Shortcut Keys.

Direct Messages

Direct Messages are like text messages. This feature lets you send a 140-character message directly to another person. No one else can see it. However, the sender and the recipient must be following each other on Twitter.

To see or send a direct message, go to your profile page and click the icon that looks like an envelope.

Favorites

If you follow a lot of people, you may want to "favorite" certain tweets created by other accounts. Conversely, from time to time other people may favorite tweets you've created.

To favorite a tweet, look for the *Favorite* link or star icon below the tweet in question. Clicking it adds the tweet to your list of favorites.

To see all of the tweets that you've marked as favorite, follow these steps:

1. Go to your profile on *twitter.com*
2. Select *More*
3. Select *Favorites*

Lists

Lists are a way of organizing Twitter accounts. Here are some examples:

- A list of people in your hometown with Twitter accounts.
- People you work with.
- Famous bands who are on Twitter.
- Thought leaders in the real estate industry.
- Comedians on Twitter.

Viewing a list's timeline displays the recent tweets from the people on the list. Here's how to see the lists that you have created or have been assigned to:

1. Go to *twitter.com*
2. Open your profile by clicking the Me icon
3. Select *More*
4. Select *Lists*

You can create a new list and add an account to it by opening a profile page and clicking on the symbol that looks like a silhouette. Then, select *Add or remove from lists*:

You do not need to follow an account to add them to a list. In addition, lists can be seen by anyone. In other words, if you create a list of Twitter accounts with funny profile pictures, not only will other people be able to see it, but the people you have added to the list will probably find it, too.

Shortcut Keys

On *twitter.com*, shortcut keys are an easy way to perform common functions, such as creating a new tweet, replying, searching, or scrolling down. Press one of the following letters or symbols on the keyboard to activate the following functions:

- **N** – Create a new tweet.
- **J** – Select the first tweet in the timeline. Subsequent presses select the next tweet in line.
- **K** – Select the previous tweet.
- **T** – Retweet selected tweet.
- **R** – Reply to selected tweet.
- **Space bar** – Scroll down. This is a great way to rapidly view recent tweets in your timeline.
- **Forward slash** – Places the cursor in the search field.

There are about a dozen more shortcut keys for more obscure or advanced functions. If you are on *twitter.com*, simultaneously press the shift and question mark keys on your keyboard to see them all.

Conclusion

In 30 minutes, you've learned the basics of Twitter, from creating an account to taking part in discussions. You now have a foundation of knowledge and practical skills that you can use to make new connections, share information, and better understand the world around you.

While it feels good knowing how Twitter works and what you can do with it, to really get value from Twitter, you have to regularly use it. After setting up your account, you should follow a few dozen interesting accounts, using the advice I gave in Chapter 3. I've also created a list of cool Twitter accounts to follow on the official book website (*twitter.in30minutes.com*).

Then start tweeting. You don't have to be fanatical, but try creating at least two tweets per day. It will help you get comfortable with Twitter, and develop your own unique voice on Twitter. Regular tweeting also will help you attract followers and engage in discussions.

Be sure to ask questions if you need help — people on Twitter generally like to help new users. Make an effort to retweet other people's interesting tweets. If you see an opportunity to help someone out on Twitter, do it. It can be as simple as answering a question or showing support in some other way.

Lastly, I welcome any reader to connect with me on Twitter. My handle is @ilamont. If you @mention this account on Twitter and let me know that you own *Twitter In 30 Minutes*, you will get a special Twitter shout-out and I will follow you back.

Thanks for purchasing *Twitter In 30 Minutes*, and I hope to see you soon on Twitter!

About the author

Twitter In 30 Minutes (2nd Edition) is authored by Ian Lamont, an award-winning business and technology journalist and digital media expert. He has written for more than a dozen online and print publications and has also served as the managing editor of *The Industry Standard*.

Lamont has released several IN 30 MINUTES guides, including *Dropbox In 30 Minutes*, *Google Drive & Docs In 30 Minutes*, and *Excel Basics In 30 Minutes*.

He is a graduate of the Boston University College of Communication and MIT's Sloan Fellows Program in Innovation and Global Leadership.

A message from the author, and a request

Writing *Twitter In 30 Minutes* was a labor of love. Since 2007, I have used Twitter to connect with people, discover information, and share photos, quips, and random observations about the world. Twitter has introduced me to new friends and experiences that I otherwise would never have had. I am happy to share what I have learned with my readers, and I hope your own Twitter journey is similarly rewarding. If you have a question about Twitter or the guide, please feel free to email me at ian@in30minutes.com.

I would also like to ask a favor. Could you take a minute to rate *Twitter In 30 Minutes (2nd edition)* and write a quick review? You can do so on these sites:

- **Amazon.com**
- **Barnesandnoble.com**
- **Goodreads.com**

An honest appraisal of the contents of *Twitter In 30 Minutes* will not only be appreciated by me, but it will also let other potential readers know what to expect.

Thanks for reading!

Ian Lamont

Bonus: Introduction to Personal Finance For Beginners In 30 Minutes (Vol. 1)

(Personal finance is a frustrating topic for millions of Americans. It's difficult to understand, there are tons of pitfalls, and at the end of the day, there never seems to be enough money to cover the things that really matter. Personal Finance For Beginners In 30 Minutes, Vol. 1 is intended to clear away the confusion and help readers develop a sensible approach toward controlling spending. To learn more about the guide, please visit personalfinance.in30minutes.com)

I'd like to introduce you to Frank, Jordan, and Stephanie. These aren't their real names, but their stories are all too real.

Frank, Jordan, and Stephanie are similar in many respects. They work at the same company, have the same job title, and have the same salary — $50,000 per year. None of them are married or have children. None of them have mortgages, crushing educational debt or outstanding loans.

You may think that their financial conditions are similar, too. $50,000 won't go that far in a city, but it's enough to live on. You may have a salary that's around the same level, or have friends or relatives who make a similar amount.

But here's the interesting thing about Frank, Jordan, and Stephanie: Even though they work the same hours and make the same amount of money, their personal finances are vastly different.

Frank's situation is the worst. Frank is always complaining that he doesn't have enough money to live on, and indeed, he was evicted from his last apartment. He takes public transportation to get to and from work, and spends less than $10 on lunch every day.

Jordan's financial situation is also precarious, but you wouldn't know it by looking at her. She dresses well, owns a nice car, and takes small vacations several times per year.

How can Jordan afford it? She can't. She keeps the creditors at bay by working a second job four nights a week, waitressing near her home. Needless to say, she can barely keep her eyes open during her day job.

Stephanie is the only one of the three who has a handle on her finances. She has her own car, manages to pay off her educational loans on time, and has even started to build a nest egg, via her employer's 401(k) plan.

Small Spending Decisions Have Big Outcomes

How can three people with identical incomes have such vastly different financial situations? Some of it relates to major purchases or household expenses, such as monthly car or rent payments. But people's financial health also depends on a myriad of small spending decisions, which, over time, can either accumulate into big shortfalls or massive savings. Understanding how this process works and making minor adjustments to maximize your lifestyle can save you thousands of dollars every year, and can help make your financial situation much stronger. It's one of the central teaching points of *Personal Finance For Beginners In 30 Minutes, Vol. 1*.

How To Lose Thousands On Lunch

Consider Frank's mealtime spending habits. Going to the cafeteria or a nearby McDonalds costs less than $10 every day. It may not sound like much, but over the course of a year, those hamburgers, McWraps, and sodas add up. In just one year, Frank spends over $1,500 on his lunch excursions.

Many of his colleagues spend less than half that amount by brown-bagging it with healthier homemade sandwiches or leftovers and only the occasional fast-food treat. Cutting down on the fast-food lunches won't eliminate Frank's financial problems, but it will make them a little easier to manage.

In Chapter 2, we'll go over how casual meals and other flexible expenses such as cable television, restaurant outings, and luxury purchases can be reduced. There are even some psychological tricks that you can use to make the cuts more bearable.

Free Money For Retirement?

At the other end of the spectrum, we have Stephanie's growing nest egg, which has been built through relatively small contributions to her company's 401(k) plan. Don't be put off by the awkward name of the 401(k) plan, which is derived from a section of the U.S. federal tax code. The plan is a simple method for saving for retirement.

Every week, Stephanie has 5% of her earnings (about $50) automatically deducted and placed in an investment account. Just like Frank's lunchtime expenses, $50 per week may not sound like much, and indeed, Stephanie doesn't even notice the difference. But over time the contributions start to add up — and in Stephanie's situation, they add up in a positive way. The weekly contributions are automatically invested in mutual funds that own baskets of stocks (such as Apple, Ford, and Disney), bonds, and other investments. Even though the money comes from her salary, the 401(k) contributions are not taxed before they are invested. They will also grow tax-free (withdrawals are taxed as ordinary income, however).

Further, like many employers, Stephanie's company offers a matching contribution of up to 5% of the employee's gross pay. In Stephanie's case, this means she is getting an additional $50 put into the mutual fund every week. That's about $2,500 in free money that's added to her investment account every year.

Stephanie's situation is covered in more detail in *Personal Finance For Beginners In 30 Minutes, Vol. 2*. I also show how Frank and Jordan are planning their retirement savings, including how much they've set aside and the types of mutual funds they have selected.

The Core Concepts Of This Guide

Frank, Jordan and Stephanie serve as real-life examples of how people on limited incomes manage their money. But there will also be explanations of basic personal finance concepts, advice on how to better manage your spending, and even tips on how to organize your records. By the time you get to the end of this book 30 minutes from now, you are going to have a different perspective on how to manage your spending and improve your long-term financial health.

The core concepts taught in this guide include:

- **Evaluating your priorities, spending, and assets** (Chapter 1, "Taking Stock Of Your Life & Finances")
- **Identifying and pruning unnecessary expenses** (Chapter 2, "Reducing Flexible Expenses")
- **Trimming necessary expenses and obligations** (Chapter 3, "Reducing Fixed Expenses")

- **Organizing and tracking your financial life** (Chapter 4, "Managing Your Accounts & Data")

Personal Finance For Beginners In 30 Minutes, Vol. 1 contains a lot of practical tips and common-sense approaches to spending. By the time you finish the last page, you will hopefully have a solid idea about how you can cut costs, better manage your debt, and establish smart spending habits that can potentially help you save thousands of dollars every year.

(To purchase a copy of Personal Finance For Beginners In 30 Minutes, *please visit personalfinance.in30minutes.com)*

Bonus: Introduction to LinkedIn In 30 Minutes

(The following bonus chapter is the introduction to LinkedIn In 30 Minutes, *by author Melanie Pinola. To download the ebook or purchase the paperback, visit the book's official website, linkedin.in30minutes.com)*

If you're serious about taking your career to the next level, you need to be on LinkedIn. In the past five years, the online career network has opened doors for millions of people, transforming the way they market themselves and enabling them to vastly expand their professional networks. In addition, companies are using LinkedIn to recruit everyone from entry-level employees to CEOs. In the next 30 minutes, this guide will show you how to best present yourself on LinkedIn and leverage other features that will help advance your career.

LinkedIn is the world's largest professional network, with more than 200 million members and counting. Hiring managers and headhunters actively use LinkedIn. Companies big and small, and millions of professionals — including executives from every Fortune 500 company — use it. You need to actively use it, too. The reason is simple: **There's no better social networking tool (or other online tool, for that matter) for furthering your career than LinkedIn.**

That's a bold statement, but research backs it up. Consider this:

- 98% of recruiters used social media to find talent in 2012, according to a Bullhorn survey. Guess which network they used to place job candidates? That's right — LinkedIn. Some 93% of the surveyed staffing professionals placed candidates through LinkedIn, compared to just 17% for Facebook and 13% for Twitter.

- Another Bullhorn survey of over 77,500 recruiters found that 48% of them post jobs on LinkedIn *and nowhere else on social media*.

That's not all. In a survey of LinkedIn users, 90% of respondents said they thought the site is useful because:

- "It helps me to connect to individuals in my industry as possible clients"

- "It is more professional than Facebook"
- "It allows me to hire people that I wouldn't regularly meet"

Ways You Can Use LinkedIn

Although many people think of LinkedIn mostly as a tool for job seekers, you can benefit substantially from using LinkedIn even if you're not ready to leave your current job. **Think of the site as a free online résumé, industry insights tool, and digital Rolodex rolled into one.**

Here are a few ways people are using LinkedIn to achieve their career goals:

- **Dan is an IT professional who's satisfied with his current job** … but he wouldn't say "no" if a more attractive opportunity presented itself! He doesn't actively check job boards, but he set up his LinkedIn profile so headhunters can easily find him.

- **Gabe is the owner of a small accounting firm**. He uses LinkedIn to promote his services to potential and current clients, discuss business strategies and general accounting topics with other LinkedIn members, and keep up with his competitors' developments.

- **Dana is a recent college graduate** who just got her first job doing graphic design. She uses LinkedIn to share — and discover — interesting information about her field, help her grow her expertise and build her professional reputation.

- **Mike has been out of work for over a year**, after huge layoffs at the manufacturing company where he used to work. LinkedIn helps him update and modernize his résumé, find companies currently hiring for his skills set, and connect with previous colleagues, employers, and classmates who could help him re-enter the workforce.

- **Jonathan is a mid-level marketing manager** who's been at the same company for the last 10 years with little advancement — and he's ready to move up! He uses LinkedIn to find relevant job openings, research and follow companies he's interested in, and find people in his network who could help with his job search.

While these people are in different stages of their careers and use LinkedIn for different purposes, they have two things in common: They're interested in maintaining or advancing their careers, and LinkedIn is central to their career development strategies. Facebook might be great for socializing and Twitter for keeping abreast of the news (or following celebrities), but LinkedIn is for your livelihood.

Note also that even though LinkedIn once targeted people working in technology-related industries and white-collar professionals, the network has since expanded to every occupation and industry. You can be a chef, a cardiologist, or a carpenter, yet still build a network and find other ways to leverage LinkedIn.

What's In This Guide

Whether you're completely new to LinkedIn or have already set up an account but are left thinking "What now?", this guide is for you. In just 30 minutes, you'll learn the basics of getting started with LinkedIn, such as how to:

- Create a strong LinkedIn profile (Chapter 1)
- Build and grow your professional network (Chapter 2)
- Use LinkedIn to find a job, stay current in your industry, and advance your career (Chapters 3 and 4)
- Make even better use of LinkedIn with power user tricks such as organizing your LinkedIn contacts and changing privacy settings (Chapter 5, and online at linkedin.in30minutes.com)

At the end of each chapter is a convenient checklist, which will help ensure that you have hit the most important steps.

By the way, if you're the type of person who cringes when someone gushes about "networking," don't worry. As a shy, card-carrying introvert, "networking" is not my favorite word either. One of the great things about LinkedIn is this isn't the same kind of networking that happens at conventions, where you're wearing a name tag, trying to meet strangers, and awkwardly attempting to make small talk. **LinkedIn is networking without the pressure**. Using the service, you can reach out to people you know — and those they know — virtually. In fact, people expect to be contacted, and others might also reach out to you. That's what the site is for!

Ready to get started? Now's a great time to find a copy of your most recently updated résumé and fire up your browser...

To learn more about LinkedIn In 30 Minutes, *or to purchase the ebook or paperback edition, please visit linkedin.in30minutes.com.*

More In 30 Minutes® Guides

What do you want to learn in 30 minutes?

Full list of titles at in30minutes.com

CPSIA information can be obtained at www.ICGtesting.com
Printed in the USA
LVOW04s1353110315

430133LV00001B/385/P